RALPH VAUGHAN WILLIAMS

SERENADE TO MUSIC

Words by Shakespeare

Vocal Score

MUSIC DEPARTMENT

OXFORD

UNIVERSITY PRESS

OXFORD
UNIVERSITY PRESS

Great Clarendon Street, Oxford OX2 6DP, England
198 Madison Avenue, New York, NY 10016, USA

Oxford University Press is a department of the University of Oxford.
It furthers the University's aim of excellence in research, scholarship,
and education by publishing worldwide in

Oxford New York

Auckland Bangkok Buenos Aires Cape Town Chennai
Dar es Salaam Delhi Hong Kong Istanbul Karachi Kolkata
Kuala Lumpur Madrid Melbourne Mexico City Mumbai Nairobi
São Paulo Shanghai Taipei Tokyo Toronto

Oxford is a registered trade mark of Oxford University Press
in the UK and in certain other countries

ISBN 978-0-19-336002-0

Engraved by Paul Broom.
Printed in Great Britain on acid-free paper by
Halstan & Co. Ltd., Amersham, Bucks.

INTRODUCTION

In January 1938 Vaughan Williams received a request from Sir Henry J. Wood for a work to be performed at a concert planned for 5 October 1938, to mark the fiftieth anniversary of his début as a conductor. Vaughan Williams replied that it would be an honour to compose something 'in your praise' and wondered if they should ask the Poet Laureate, John Masefield, for a text. Wood replied on 25 January that he did not want anything in praise of himself but rather 'a choral work that can be used at any time and for any occasion. I would not think of asking you to write a work that might only be used the once, which would naturally be the case were it written round myself.' Wood later suggested a work for sixteen singers who had sung many times with him at festivals and the Promenade Concerts. Vaughan Williams reported this to his friend Ursula Wood (who in 1953 was to become his second wife), adding that he had always wanted to set the Jessica and Lorenzo scene (Act V, Scene 1) from Shakespeare's *The Merchant of Venice*. 'Eight Jessicas and eight Lorenzos?' she asked. 'No, just a little bit for each voice.' Vaughan Williams sent Wood the manuscript of the work on 2 June. The sixteen singers were:

Sopranos	**Altos**	**Tenors**	**Basses**
Isobel Baillie	Margaret Balfour	Parry Jones	Norman Allin
Stiles Allen	Muriel Brunskill	Heddle Nash	Robert Easton
Elsie Suddaby	Astra Desmond	Frank Titterton	Roy Henderson
Eva Turner	Mary Jarred	Walter Widdop	Harold Williams

The parts allotted to each of these singers are indicated in the score by their initials, including their participation in choral passages. It is uncanny how Vaughan Williams captured the vocal characteristics of all sixteen in such brief phrases and we are fortunate that their artistry is preserved in the recording made a few days after the first performance. Who that heard them could fail to recognise Heddle Nash in 'Look how the floor of heaven is thick inlaid with patines of bright gold'? Or Eva Turner at 'How many things by season season'd are to their right praise and true perfection'? Or Isobel Baillie's ethereal 'Of sweet harmony' with which the work ends? Yet the marvel is that when later singers perform these passages they seem by alchemy to absorb the spirit of the originals while retaining their own individuality.

The *Serenade* can be performed by four solo singers (soprano, alto, tenor, and bass) and chorus or all the solo parts may be sung in chorus. There is also a version for orchestra without voices, made at Wood's suggestion in 1939. As Wood hoped, the *Serenade* has outlived the occasion for which it was written and is widely regarded as one of the most beautiful and inspired of all settings of Shakespeare.

Michael Kennedy
2008

SERENADE TO MUSIC

How sweet the moonlight sleeps upon this bank!
Here will we sit and let the sounds of music
Creep in our ears: soft stillness and the night
Become the touches of sweet harmony.
. . . Look how the floor of heaven
Is thick inlaid with patines of bright gold:
There's not the smallest orb that thou behold'st
But in his motion like an angel sings,
Still quiring to the young-ey'd cherubins;
Such harmony is in immortal souls;
But, whilst the muddy vesture of decay
Doth grossly close it in, we cannot hear it.
Come, ho! and wake Diana with a hymn:
With sweetest touches pierce your mistress' ear,
And draw her home with music.
I am never merry when I hear sweet music.
The reason is, your spirits are attentive:
. . . The man that hath no music in himself,
Nor is not mov'd with concord of sweet sounds,
Is fit for treasons, stratagems and spoils;
The motions of his spirit are as dull as night,
And his affections dark as Erebus;
Let no such man be trusted.
Music! Hark! . . . It is the music of the house.
Methinks it sounds much sweeter than by day.
Silence bestows that virtue on it . . .
How many things by season season'd are
To their right praise and true perfection!
Peace, ho! The moon sleeps with Endymion,
And would not be awak'd!
. . . Soft stillness and the night
Become the touches of sweet harmony.

(William Shakespeare, *c.*1564–1616, *The Merchant of Venice*)

Serenade to Music

William Shakespeare (*c.*1564–1616)

R. VAUGHAN WILLIAMS

Orchestral material is available on hire from the Publisher's Hire Library, or appropriate agent.

Printed in Great Britain

OXFORD UNIVERSITY PRESS, MUSIC DEPARTMENT, GREAT CLARENDON STREET, OXFORD, OX2 6DP

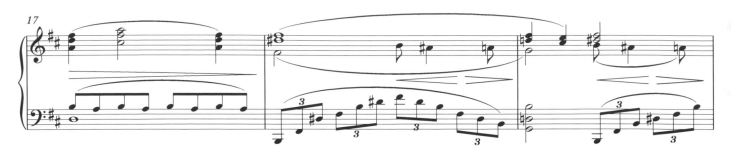

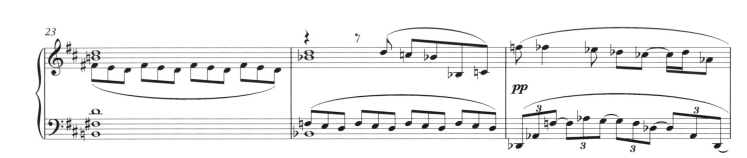

Poco animato

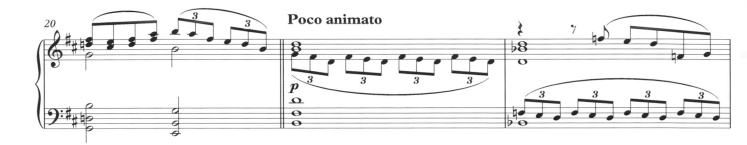

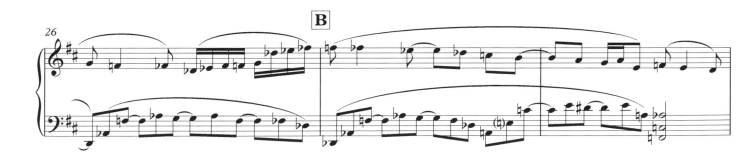

B

poco rit.　　tempo primo

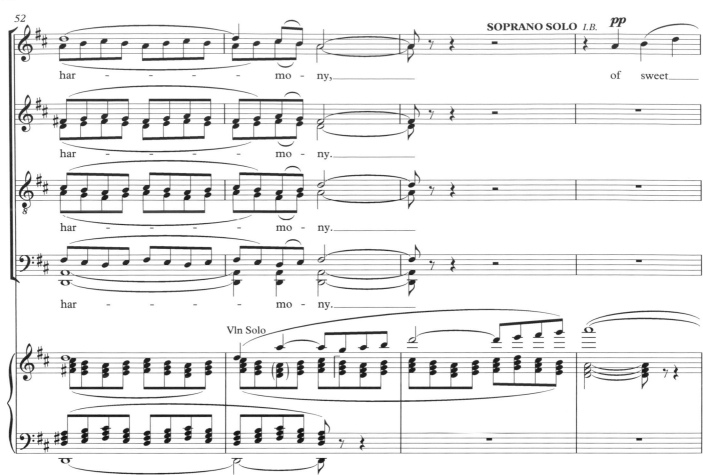

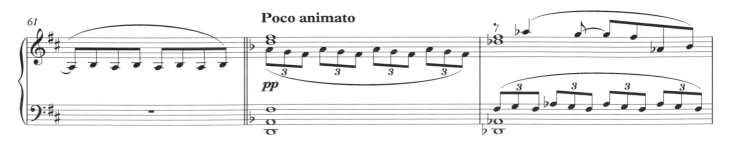

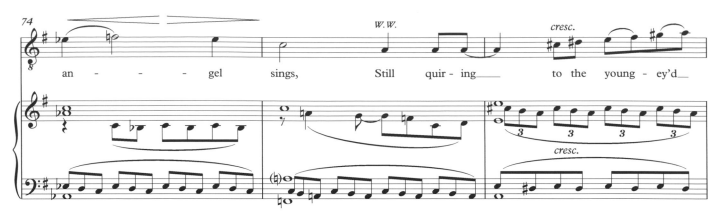

an - - - gel sings, Still quir-ing____ to the young-ey'd

che - - - - - - - ru - bins;

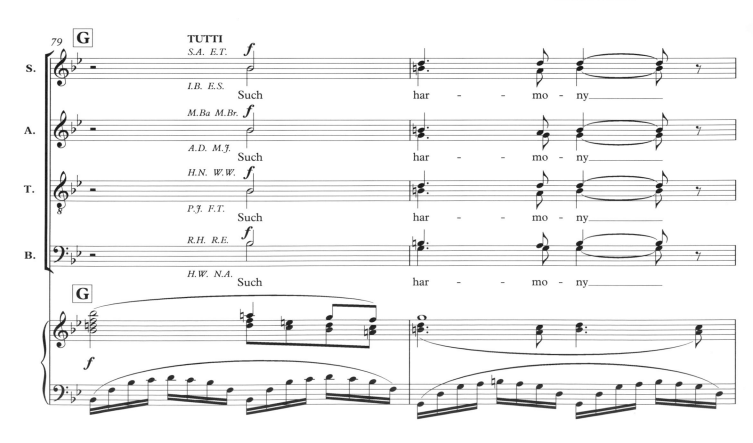

Such har - - mo - ny

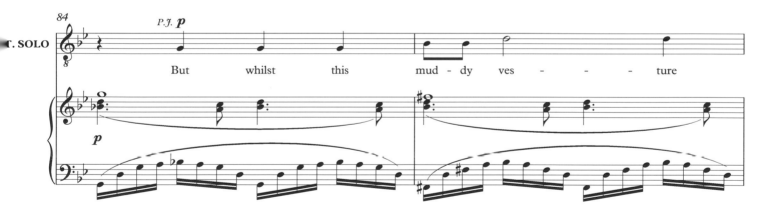

14

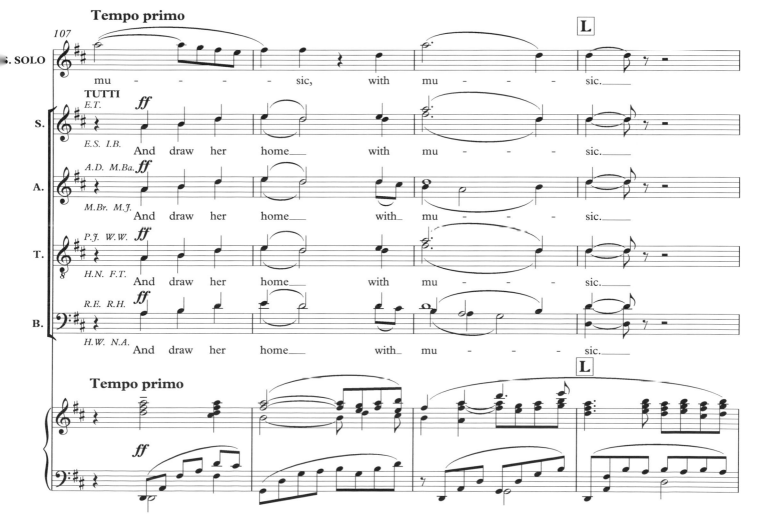

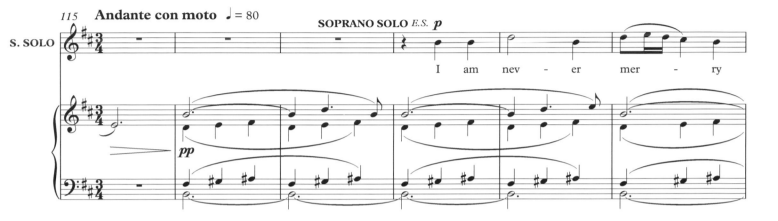

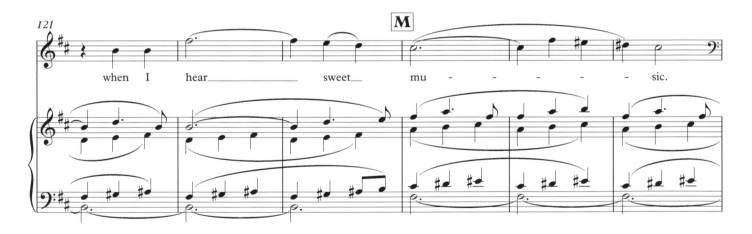

The man_____ that hath no mu-sic_____ in him-

-self,_____ Nor is not mov'd with con-cord of sweet____

_____ sounds,____ Is fit for trea - sons,

stra - ta - gems and spoils;____

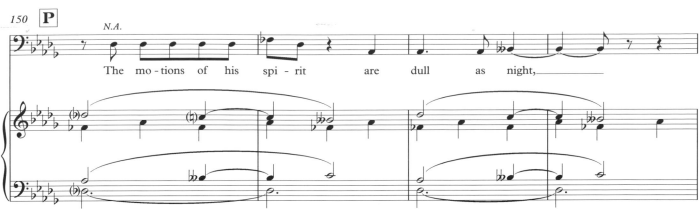

The mo-tions of his spi-rit are dull as night,_____

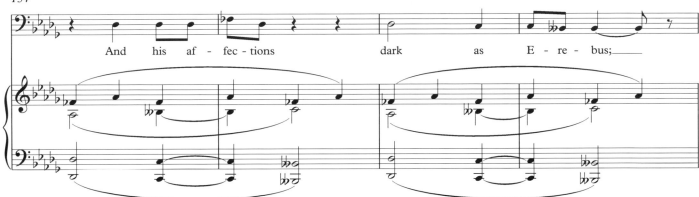

And his af-fec-tions dark as E-re-bus;_____

Let no such man be trust-ed.

Let no such man be trust-ed.

Let no such man be trust-ed.

Let no such man be trust-ed.

Q

Tempo primo (ma poco animato)

A. SOLO

M.Br. *f*   *poco rit.*

Mu - sic!   Hark!

Tempo primo

It   is   your   mu - sic   of   the   house.

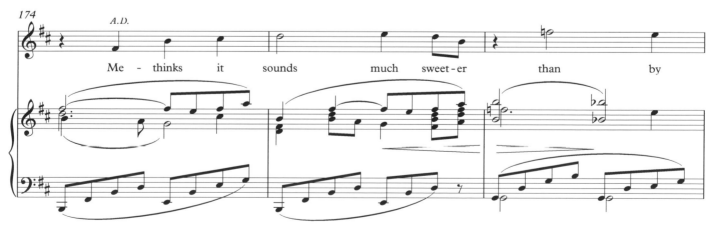

Me - thinks   it   sounds   much   sweet-er   than   by

To their right praise and

true per - fec - tion!

S

ALTO SOLO M.Ba. *p*

Peace, ho!

The moon sleeps

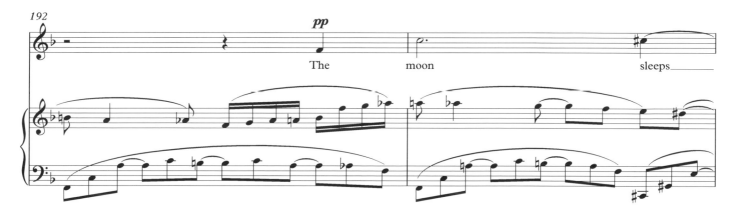

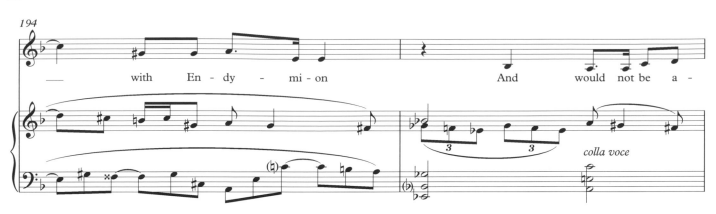

with En - dy - mi - on
And would not be a -

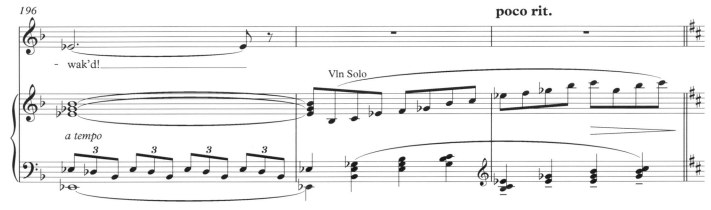

poco rit.

- wak'd!

Vln Solo

a tempo

Tempo primo

S.

TUTTI
I.B S.A.

ppp

E.S. E.T.

Soft still - -

A.

ppp

Soft still - -

T.

H.N. F.T.

ppp

P.J. W.W.

Soft still - -

B.

R.E. R.H.

ppp

H.W. N.A.

Soft still - -

Tempo primo

pp

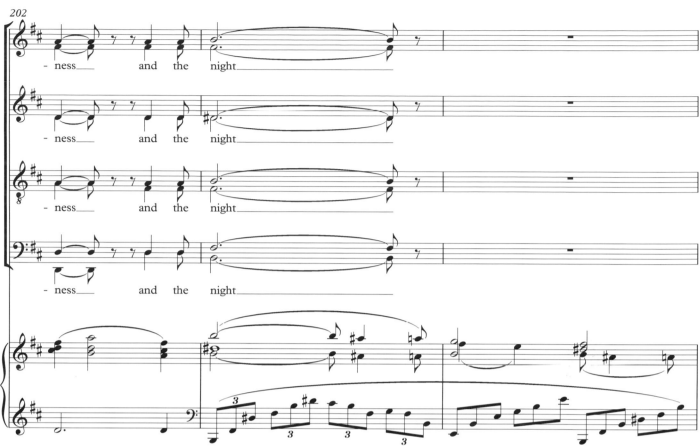

24

Music engraved by Paul Broom.
Printed in England by Halstan & Co. Ltd., Amersham, Bucks.